Fire in Wild Wood

Written by Wes Magee

Illustrated by Val Biro

Nesta and Ned were little dragons.

One day they flew to Wild Wood.

They saw Big Bad Dragon in Wild Wood.

Big Bad Dragon was cross.
'I will make a fire in Wild Wood,'
he said.
He blew fire at the grass.
He blew fire at the trees.

Wild Wood was on fire.

Ned and Nesta saw the fire.

'We will stop Big Bad Dragon,'
said Nesta.

'Stop!' said Nesta.

'Stop!' said Ned.

But Big Bad Dragon did not stop.

He blew fire at Nesta and Ned.

Nesta and Ned flew off.

They went to see the spiders.

'Can we have your cobweb?'
said Nesta.

'Yes,' said the spiders.

Nesta and Ned put the cobweb
in the trees.
Big Bad Dragon saw the cobweb.
'What is that?' said Big Bad Dragon.
'Come and find out,' called Ned.

Big Bad Dragon ran into the cobweb.
The cobweb fell on Big Bad Dragon.
'Help! Help!' he said.

'Got him!' said Nesta.

'Got him!' said Ned.

Big Bad Dragon was very cross.

Nesta and Ned got the cobweb.

'Come on Big Bad Dragon,' they said.

'Home you go!'

Nesta and Ned flew off with
Big Bad Dragon.
They flew to Creepy Castle.

'Down you go!' said Nesta and Ned.
And Big Bad Dragon fell down

down

down.